AF251603

Don Cushman

**ISBN:** 0-916300-02-1

**Library of Congress Cataloguing in Publication Data:**

Published by
GALLIMAUFRY
359 Frederick
San Francisco, Ca. 94117




Printed in an edition of 500
by Don Cushman
at the West Coast Print Center
1975

# JIM AND THE EVIL

## Don Cushman

*GALLIMAUFRY*
*San Francisco, California*
*1975*

When shores remind me
of the inner softness of thighs
and I have learned the dreams
of starfish and mollusks,
during those fluted moments
before a small death
when my life flashes before me
like dancers on a glass lake,
it is then that Jim appears and says,
*I am what you are always coming back to.*

Jim, I say, you are the essence
abstracted from sorrow,
you are the only clear explanation
of the obvious,
the mask I wear on the darkest
night of the year.

Jim says, *I am the stone
that reverberates through the water.*

Jim, If I say walk one mile with me
walk two, and when I am changing faces
stand behind my eyes, lift your
bandaged hands to your bandaged face
and shout, **Emerge!**

**SURVIVAL NECESSITIES**


Road windings
briar paths
branch tunnels.
Jim is seated calmly
by a stream.
*Why*, he asks,
*do you cough stones?*
I sag
knees doubling.
*Why do you think*
*you are lost?* he asks.
Because, I say,
I thought there was a path.
Jim says, *If crows fly in circles*
*that is their business.*

My soul contracts like a watchspring.
I tell myself on nights
such as these,
Time and my soul depend
on the tension of watchsprings.
Jim begins to walk very fast.
I fall behind. I am caught in a storm.
At first I feel a mist,
followed by a hollow thud.
Soon it is dark and I am not young
and the weeks and years have blown by
and my soul has constricted and unwound
a thousand times and I sleep on the run
and doze when I think I am awake.
Jim is always just out of earshot.
I think I am following you, I say.
This time storm has obscured everything.

And I run no longer sure
it is Jim I am following
or if I have developed a fondness for running
a fondness for the lung pain
for the muscle screams
for the survival necessities.
Jim, I say, will I ever catch you?
Jim says, *The heartbeat is the sound
of an animal at bay, the path wears the runner smooth,
the ribcage makes a fine prison.*

Jim is bruised,
beleaguered,
beset by hounds,
happy in hiding,
camouflaged.
*The hunted*, he says,
*enjoys the necessity*
*of the hunt.*

Jim, I say, I don't
find myself
inside my skin.
Jim says, *The lair is the secret*
*of the fox.*
I say, My days are a blur
of inactivity.
I work and the work
does not disappear.
Lost in the machinery
invisible in the eyes
of friends
blind to myself
I walk.
Less than humble
afraid of discomfort
half in love with easeful
catastrophe
stripped of my youth
avoiding mirrors
I walk into the husk
of the future.
*The hunter*, Jim mumbles
out of breath, cornered,
*who is his own prey*
*never lacks for hounds.*

Jim hides in the shadows
of a bakery.
He lounges unassailable,
figmentary.
He reads from a microfilm
psalter.
**Proud vegetarian wisemen
will queue in the distance
and their hunger will flower
in its season. The man
who looks into the distance
overlooks himself on the way.
The scorpion is gentle
with her lover.
A flood will be contained
in a tear.**

I am hurrying to work,
my survival kit
under my arm.
I sing from my hymnal
as I run:
A child is smaller than a man,
a man is smaller than his self.
His daydreams are larger
than his essence.

For a moment I pause.
We are pinioned
by the points of a compass.
Jim is dark, desolate.
*The answer will not be found
in the question.*

## STONE HORSES

Jim is lost, his spirit flagged down,
quashed like a supoena.
He finds me painting lanterns in a cave.
*I have looked for you*
*in all the old haunts;*
*storm drain, deserted turbine,*
*bridge strut.*
*I found your body easily.*
*Nightmare enraptured,*
*your eyes glazed over with choices.*
*It was your luminosity that evaded me.*
*It wandered darkened spillways*
*and flood swollen levees.*
*You have shouldered your sadness*
*like a knapsack packed with shadows.*

Jim, I say, The night is fog-shrouded,
a secreting of stars, way obscuring.
I turn all the corners, looking over my shoulder.
I am either walking toward or away, my dark image either
hunted or hunting, my death stationary grinning
from doorways.
I see tears streaming down the faces of my unborn children.
I see lovers turn to face me. Their eyes become clouds.
I see stone horses blinking in parks.
I see unknown rivers rushing through
the midnights of a secret existence.
I see the unchecked rushing of my youth
through the dry oblivion of sleep and survival.

I see the horsemen frozen to saddles of stone horses.
I create rooms, feelings of self-fossilization,
memories of eyes of bodies that refused to meet
as outside ourselves, outside the metered flow of emotions
and circumstances our lives thrashed about
in search of a dream calming emotion
that might slow the rush of our bodies toward death.

Jim is resting on a boulder. Or a boulder is resting on Jim.
His eyes reveal the pain he takes on with each new love.
*Everything is provided*, he says,
*The room  the meal  the knives.*
*What you consume will be determined*
*by your hunger.*

# THE SECRET AGENT

Jim climbs down from the skylight
disguised as Francis of Assissi.
A starling perches on his shoulder.
He shows me his hands
burned with the harsh stigmata of solitude.

Jim, I say,
I have just dreamt that all the friends
I have never made married each other
and I swept up the rice
and someone broke into my house
and smashed everything.

Jim says,
*I am a secret agent.*
*I search for the code names.*
*Decode the messages of dreams.*
*Lounge in doorways my ear to the wall.*
*I steal only the files marked top secret.*

Jim, I say,
I have become the doorman of the lost cabaret
I am walled in, my eyelids epoxied
I stare into my own darkness.
I am studying the execution of the spirit.
Blindfold sadness the midnight is tattooed
to my forehead.
Lovers spill their nightmares like fine wine
until they are stained with secrets and
the whisperers call my name in the darkness.

Jim says,
*A spy falls in love with the idea of the secret.*
*Searches for whatever is too deep to find.*
*The clues are everywhere but useless.*

Jim, The night slices through me.
To be lost in it is a way of solving the maze.
Jim, the long vine of solitude twists itself around me.
But its flowers are as beautiful as you can imagine.

## THE OTHER LIFE

OK, I'm ready to reopen
the debate on the other life.
Lights please.
Jim steps from the trapdoor
behind the crown of thorns.
I roll back the stone
from the cave of shadows.

I say, I have ridden subways
that had no destinations.
I have tumbled endlessly
through the cylinder of dreams.

Jim says, *even the road that
leads nowhere must be taken.*

But I am constantly undressing
and I am never naked.
I mark failure as the only
point of embarcation.
I watch the dead for signs
of the great disappearing act.

Jim says, *the wall and the stone wings*

Yes, I say,
there is nothing to affirm
and nothing to deny,
thinking one thing
I become someone else.
My shadow cannot keep up with me,
my wife sifts through the ashes
in search of my real body.

She has made a statue of me
she keeps in the refrigerator,
a statue with faces that are endless doors.

Jim says, *a microscopic web
stretches from one end of you
to the other. It is woven in one piece,
a glint of silver in the moonlight.*

But I have forgotten
the touch of delicate women.
I cannot run my fingers
over the soft weave.
I have moved out of my shell
into the tidal wave of my body.

Jim says, *the seed buried in the wind
the salt invisible in the wave.*

## YOU TOO, EVEL KNIEVEL

Jim leaps through a window
dressed like a daredevil
crash helmet parachute
ripcord held firmly
between his teeth.
He walks in a crouch
his arms outstretched.
A pair of ostentatious wings
fashioned from doves' feathers
and the cloaks of madmen
flutter indecisively on his shoulders.

Jim, I say,
I stand on the ledges of penthouses
I walk the wires without a net
I hang from the minute hands of huge clocks
I float over the abyss
I toy with it.
Jim says, *Our lives come to such small differences.*

Jim, I say,
It is so easy to throw
life away for nothing but
the feeling of tantalizing
death for nothing but the feeling
of your insides turned to a molten sea
blood pouring from nose and mouth
eyes pressed back into your head
everything red blood-drenched prismed
consciousness hanging by the unraveled
threads of a spider's web.
Jim says, *Our lives come to such small differences.*

Yes, I say,
Every moment hangs on a cruel balance
I have felt myself poised
over the abyss between our lives
I have felt the g-forces
the accelerations and reentries
through the space our loves create
I have been broken
thrown through the air
by the slightest miscalculations.
I have dreamt of flight
strapped the wings lovingly
on my back I have flown
too near the sun I have leapt
the innumerable shadow
danced naked over the silvered glass
I have heard the Siren's song
have fell under its spell
yes, all this I have felt
in a glance between lovers
in the darkness of 3 o'clock
in the morning in the cockpit
of my dreams which leave me
broken my bones poked through
my skin my parachute still
unopened on my back.

I look up and Jim is dangling
upsidedown from a flagpole
he is straightjacketed chain-enmeshed
struggling to escape
*Our lives*, he says, *come to such small differences.*

Jim and I go to see the psychic wonders.
A bald man with one blue eye and one brown eye
levitates before a chessboard.
He moves the queen simply by focusing
his attention on her.
A crowd of poets and merchant marines
shred their plane tickets.
Jim is not impressed.
*You are dripping with sweat.*
*Your eyes look like ashtrays after a party.*
*Your body as crumpled as an empty cigarette package*
*and all you have done is push a piece of ivory*
*around a board. Outside mad winds are blowing children*
*into replicas of the nightmares of their ancestors.*
*Outside this room ineptitude masquerades as evil*
*and civilization is a way of creating refugees*
*and we feel the sadness until it becomes*
*a skin tattooed with meaningless dates*
*until it is so much easier not to be real*
*until our shadows are more real than our dreams.*
The bald man with one blue eye and one brown eye
stares at a key till it bends, writes FUCK THE WORLD
on a blackboard with invisible chalk.
Jim loses his patience,
throws the chessmen out the window,
straightens the key, erases the blackboard.
*The power was not invented for your benefit.*
*The spider needs a point outside itself to spin the web.*
*Damn you that you can turn a galaxy into a parlor trick.*
The bald man with one blue eye and one brown eye
goes on unconcerned. Bunches of grapes, counterfeit twenty
dollar bills, concertinas, bicycle pumps, antique garters,
bluechip stocks move around the room.
He looks pleased with himself.
Everything that can be bent or twisted fills the room.
Paradoxes form from reinforcing rods.

There are coat hangers, politicians, lampstands,
bookshelves, lovers, antennas.
The bald man with one blue eye and one brown eye
is surrounded by an immense sea of lightbulbs.
Jim is seated comfortably on a pile of old truck tires.
*You will*, he says, *find the meaning of "Cat's breath".*
*Your glass will break in your hand,*
*food will taste like the ashes of nightmares.*
*Your dreams will echo like warehouses*
*and the one who sees the dream*
*will find you screaming*
*and not lift a finger to help.*

# JIM AND THE EVIL

Jim and I are home,
comfortable, some say
virtuous.
Suddenly a chair flies
through the room
smelling of gardenias
and sulphur
Jim says,
*The chair tires of the floor.*
Knives slice the air
of midnight.
There are swordfights
of invisible but superb
swordsmen on the staircase.
Jim says,
*A sharpening wind.*
In the morning
there are broken plates
dead fish that have swum
a thousand years
to break their hearts here.
There are birds
miners take into the earth;
antler down, rose petals,
love letters, the dust
of disintegrated incantations,
starched and stolen chasubles
from the bodies of renegade archbishops.
Jim, I say, I fear the evil.
He answers,
*This is not the evil.*
*Hunger is evil.*
*Homelessness is evil.*

*Life without passion is evil.*
*A husband without a mistress is evil.*
*The ignorant who wield power are evil.*
*The fear of dreams is evil.*
A cat that is being wrung out
like a sponge floats over out heads.
Night and day blend into demonic twilight.
bruises appear and disappear on my body
like Javan Atolls.
Shadows prepare shadowy meals.
Dishes burst apart and reassemble themselves.
Jim says,
*Our aimlessness is evil.*
*Survival without beauty is evil.*
*A nation that forgets art is evil.*
*Generals who unite under the tent*
*of death are evil.*
*The soldiers who obey them are evil.*
*The rest of us who pave their way*
*with our thoughts are evil.*
*A house without laughter is evil.*

Awake after a thousand nights
of insomnia, listening to the footsteps
of invisible houseguests,
listening to the clatter of furniture
and crockery, listening to the mad dances
of the silverware,
I say, Jim, if this is not the evil, what is it?
Jim says,
*A restless existence.*

jim wimpled
in whiteface
in his hand a torch
                burgeoning
        on the wild
a storm swirls
out of the north
the sky forms a message
a warning
jim, concerned,
mimes the macabre
possibilities of the future
he mimes the drowsiness
of troops before surrender
an ecstatic dream of cataclysmic changes
jim is faced with a mirror
one hand draws it closer
one hand pushes it away
                now he is asleep
a somnambulist in a white coat
now he is unconcerned
now he is a devoted gardner
planting dead seeds in the frozen earth
now he is a priest in a deserted bombed out
church performing a useless ritual by rote
into the emptiness
                he mimes the
        radioactive dreams
does the dance of the wildcat well
the minuet of armaments the waltz
of friends who glide past each other
but refuse to touch and the dance of lovers
who touch and move away
                the tear in the corner
        of his eye says
idiots
would tell
better
tales.

day
a thousand hands invent iron keyboards
windows are clogged with dreamers and suicides
bartenders, mailmen, and private investigators
parachute through skylights
trailing tickertape and subpoenas
pinned to the dentist's chair, numbed
bludgeoned into silence
having completed the whirling hermit's
dance of insomniacs
when my soul subpoenas my body
and peace dissolves like analgesic tablets,
suddenly it is calm
at the hour when lunch and madness coincide
when we beat our hands with stones to feel
and get drunk to ease the pain
at the hour when no one flies into himself
when we are all on the streets walking
as if there were at least an interim destination
suddenly at midday i am at peace
with the minute slab of the universe
i pretend to understand

a child plays with the lens of a camera
for a moment it focuses perfectly
such a moment (we live from one to the next)
is inexplicable
or as jim, who takes a job as a travel agent
explains, *when it's raining, don't hurry.*
*It's raining everywhere.*

## ARIZONA JIM

Jim is tough, his skin a relief map of Arizona.
Picks his teeth with a claw hammer.
Lights his matches on his eyelids.
Cracks his eggs with a hatchet.
There are whole avenues he has homesteaded
and feelings he has slept off like cheap wine.

Jim, I say,
An old man with my face is sitting on a decrepit
porch. His face is beaten with dreams.
Memories crawl over him like insects.

Jim says, *There are places that are all road
and cactus an all you got for company is the fly in yr ear.*

But time wheezes and spits
and already there is a part of me
arranging that chair to catch the light
looking off into the distance
spinning a web of sadness so fine
it reaches back to touch me now
because it is so hard living
for that old man, giving him something
to remember, giving him a pattern he might recognize
something more than a young man's writhings
something more than all the midnights
strung like black pearls
because I know that no matter what I do
he'll spin his own goddam web
and he'll kill all the parts of me he doesn't want
and I still, like all the madmen before me,
want to leave a feeling  an image  a memory
so complete even that foolish old man won't miss it.

Jim says, *Man I met this chick hadn't seen for years*
*I sez hi she sez I member you maybe cept we wuz*
*drunk an maybe baby we done somethin cept we wuz thinkin*
*bout someone else an I sez yea baby*
*an we waved an jes kept on goin.*

Jim, all these faces learning to stare
all the dreams packed like overnight bags
the love cries the extravagant laughter
the wanderings  the train stations  the caresses
the shadow punches  the running battles
the reveries
the shell polishing itself with the sound of the ocean.

Jim says, *Man, you know it jes blow my mind,*
*all the streets out there have names.*

## IBN EL JIM

I find him in the garage.
He is surrounded by vials.
Everything is coming to a boil.
He is wearing a green eyeshade
and an overcoat fashioned
from the skin of the last bear.

Jim, I say, you have changed.
*Tell me*, he says,
*can you distinguish the color of the wine*
*from the color of the glass?*
I don't know, I say,
I am lost between the image in the photograph
and the image in my dreams.
I dream of trains that pull away from me.
I dream of the dark but familiar corridors I run through
because I cannot find my room in the darkness.
Knives call me by name.
I wear everything inside out.
When I hear the sirens in the midnight
I know they are playing my song.
I say I am sorry to the salad the meat
and the bread just in case.

Jim says, *Salt sulphur mercury*
*rubbing your hands together is a kind of fire*
*The alchemist's gold longs to be lead.*
*A lion may crouch forever in its own shadow.*

I pace in circles, my hat pulled down
over my eyes. I crash into bookcases,
whiskey stills, armchairs. Stumble over villains
that turn out to be statues.
Jim ignores me. Goes about his experiments.
*A song*, he says, *is hiding in the silence.*

I take my hat off and run backwards
and think of the past. I thrash about.
My neck stiffens from looking over my shoulder
and still my thoughts are rear view mirrors
and I see the crash victims holding their heads
and I hear the sirens that are playing my song
and I wrap myself in bandages just in case.
Knives smile. My razor refuses to testify.
Jim holds up a new vaccine.
*The cure*, he says, *is a form of the disease.*

jim and I are at a bar
pouring whiskeys on blank sheets of paper
a man who has drunk enough to know better
asks jim **Why do you write?**
jim laughs like a bishop hearing confessions in a brothel
*I don't write…he does.*
*ask him.*
the drunk slurs, **ok hotshot why do you write?**

and I begin to writhe, stammer,
**ok hotshot why?**
jim grins like a bullfighter
I say
because the midnights are armed with cattleprods
because there is a moment in a dream when you
are falling and you can't catch yourself
and you can't turn back
because there are nights when you had to keep talking
because you were afraid to fall asleep
because you want to have the last word
because it thickens the plot
because you are on the road and you don't know a song
because no one ever told you
you can't dance without moving your feet
because you have broken loves
and you have been broken by love
and you no longer know
what to call happiness or even comfort
except you seem to run away from them
and you choose the pain because of the hard sounds
and you walk the wire with someone on your shoulders
because you have worked and you have seen into lives
and think you have felt the adrenalin
pumped through your veins

because you come back again and again
for the challenge, the complexity of the act
the ripcord, the wildcat well
the drunk is asleep on the bar

jim stares into the empty glass
*it is not the whiskey that has made me drunk*
*but the process of emptying*
*so many glasses.*

He walks into the deserted courtroom. His eyes wander over some inner strategy. They narrow a second as something falls silently into place. It is the case of the Ravaged Midnight. Stones secreted in library vaults, music blaring uncontrollably under the coffin strewn altar, naked widows running through the fields of the long deserted manor, disappearing coins, legendary and perfect fireplace pokers, thousands of whorling vortical fingerprints. Lt. Tragg lumbers in with his theatrics, looks over the heads of the jury, confident. He has a coin in his pocket, guilty faces on both sides. Perry recalls a witness. It is Jim, who has taken a job as an accountant in a brothel. **Were you not on the night of the fourteenth seen speaking to someone in the shadows of the darkened marquee? Were you not in fact in love with the neice of the accused and did you not conspire to defraud yourself of the millions left in trust by the retired counterfitter of lost masterpieces?** Jim says, *The truth is illusive. We substitute a pattern of fact.* Murmurs in the courtroom. Seven men in overcoats confess to everything. Afterwards back in the office, Perry explains. **It was the countess' false eyelash and the painter's lost brush that became the clues to the flickering light from a thousand candles.** As Jim said after the trial, *The innocent have no need of such small details. The guilty in their haste overlook them.*

I say
all seven candles
have gone out
Jim says
*you're in love*
I say
when I dream
of a door
there are two
when I open one
I see a sea of doors
Jim says
*open the other*
I open it and see
a basket of black fish
and two priests
dining on the moon
Jim says
*life is difficult*
and I see you standing
in a grove of cypress
you open a door
in your side
and I see
a crow pecking at your heart
Jim says
*but love, love is so simple.*

## KILL JIM

The word goes out. Whispers from a thousand doorways
from derelict autos rusting in backyards
hidden in headlines, spells itself in the bottoms of teacups.
Finally a man sidles up after a reading
dressed in hipboots and carrying a sandbag.
The word is out he says. **Kill Jim.**
On moonless nights assassins roam the streets,
one thought frozen to their eyelids. **Kill Jim.**
I nail the windows shut. I cut the phone wires.
Live in the cellar.

Bombers idle on runways. Silos glisten with a dark lustre.
Races of innocent bystanders are massacred.
Blank faced men stare into the void. **Kill Jim.**
Passions are invented, pretexts.
Lovers wear bullet proof vests. A tax on shadows is levied.
I find my self once more lost in the human, lost in
someone else's system, and still the days invent litanies
of madness and still our lives disappear easily
and the walls struggle to compose a warning.

Old wars stare grisled from balconies.
Tears are anticlimaxes. Politicians brandish blackjacks
at news conferences called to say **Kill Jim.**
I find Jim. He is practicing an interior trapeze act.
He mumbles, *Balance. Timing. Concentration.*
Jim, I say, Time is of the essence.
*No*, he says, *it is not.*
But they are arming your friends and your enemies.
Tanks have replaced stationwagons.
and I see him flying, doing a double somersault, catching himself.
He grins slyly, *We must find something to do while we wait, yes?*

Jim comes around
hasn't been here for years
he steps out of the mechanical sunlight
there is a breeze in his passing
rustling of leaves deep in the forest
immense redwoods wave imperceptibly
release showers of needles, filaments of daydreams

Jim, I say,
everywhere I step
alarms sound
the day has become a howling siren
helicopters hover over me
I am put to sleep by firemen
my clothes arranged by the bedside
for emergencies
doors are locking frantically
the sounds are awesome
above them I hear the bombays slam shut,
hydraulic whispers, whistling lullabyes

Jim says,
*the candlelight dims behind the miasmic curtain*

I say
at night
waves of death wash over the waking man
there are times when it is not good to be a man
a hand yanks me back into the mist
a part of myself schools itself in fear
fear that is the dark shroud of ancestral memory
the imaginary line where the unknown begins

Jim says,
*the oyster dreams incessantly of the pearl*

## THE TABLES TURNED

Jim comes to me and says,
*When I see the black crow on my sill*
*I know the day will grow darker in eclipse.*
*When I feel the earth tremble beneath me*
*I know the lost races are shuddering*
*because they are alone with their secrets.*
*When I dream of a planet it is Mars*
*because fear and death race around me ceaselessly.*
*When I feel the skin of her breasts*
*I know I have found the lost continents.*
*When my thoughts grow darker than the light from a black hole*
*when fear blackens the inside of my face*
*when the blind barber offers me eternity*
*and loneliness with the same hand*
*when the beauty of the imagination merges with the terror*
*when the diver struggles to the surface in vain*
*when the spirit sees itself for what it is*
*I know that dark furrow in my hand called the future.*

My mirror bursts into tears.
I shout all I have learned.
The pearl is a burden to the oyster.

# MACHINE MORNING

I put on overcoat, galoshes.
Drive a steamshovel to work.

Jim says, *Ample protection.*

I gnash coffee cups for breakfast
and scrape a handful of ashes for lunch.

Jim says, *Callouses will suffice for friends.*

The boss coughs and spits rivets through sheet metal.
Machines scream a constant seraphic protest.

Jim says, *The moment will wait for you to wince before it moves on.*

Black dust from the moth wings of nightmares flies through me.
My daydreams pound at me like a drop forge.

Jim says, *Your mirror reflects a darker purpose.*

And I will an explosion that will blow this roof off
that will carry this machine whining over the rooftops.

Jim says, *Tears will substitute for reasons.*

Noon arrives like a shipwreck.
I wash my hands violently and well.

Jim says, *There are bruises for which there is no balm.*

# WALT WHITMAN REST HOME

Jim is suddenly old, begins to mumble to himself, gives advice to everyone, wheels himself into the whirlpool, his naked leathery body sprawled out like a sign post in the desert. He says, *I began to tell them the secrets I had learned, the secrets of disguise, of work, of waiting for the right moment. I told them that life was like leaping from a sheer Peruvian cliff for Timex. I told them that the butterfly longs for the cocoon. They feed me menthol and when I am thirsty they lock up my whiskey. I began to shout, 'time is the prisoner of clocks'. I slept in nests, gathered discarded remnants of the earth for my bed, danced with the false messiah of the Holiday Inn. My friends forgot me and my family put me here in the Walt Whitman rest home. Here where an erection is the last status symbol, where the carpet is the beautiful uncut hair of nylon, where my memory slips over the cornfields, the desolate cemetaries, over the platoons of military graves to the river, to the long salmon run of my youth. I dissolve in the minutiae of my life; the forest at five o'clock in the morning, the solemn curve of her breast. I told them death has no horror. An old man slips into his youth. They sent me long mimeographed letters on religious holidays, consulted with my doctor about the causes and cures of old age. I, swearing by the great bearing in the hub of the universe, 'this is no country for old men', began to imagine the placid face of death. As I slipped into the water, the crystal shattered on my wrist.*

# THE CHILD WEAVERS

*Say it*, Jim shouts.
I try but the words disguise themselves
as shadows in raincoats lowering at bus stops.
*Say it*
and a winch drags me back through the avenues
of faces, through a hall of voices.
Everyone is trying to laugh.
Laughter that is more like a bark.
Jim pushes aside a manhole cover and says
*Say it*
I try but history is not real enough to run from.
Jim needs an excuse to cry. Peels onions for a living.
*Say it*, he grumbles.
I sit outside in the shade of the artillery plants,
my fingers stained with the soot of words.
Day after day the child weavers weave the sad tapestries
and the mad search for the hands that work the shuttle.
And I go to bed every night and fall asleep to the same thought
over and over, **Jim will find your lovers in their dreams.**
Jim appears in a flock of opal butterflies.
*Say it*, he says.

The power is to know the name of the stone
from which you will not budge.
The night sweats, the scar tissue, the badly knit bones,
the work that is a long ancestral scream that grows louder,
the fingerprints that have become your calling card,
the old trunks of photographs, the long leavetakings
that are like assassinations of the spirit, the double helix of sadness
These are what you will know,
the ashes from which to scrape together an offering.

**BUSINESS**


I never wander. I'm on wheels
that always are turning.
The scenery moves past;
boulevard, elevator, will call.

O the lovesongs of the multitudinous
jackhammers. I'm having a wall phone
installed on my hip. Making love reminds
me of carbon paper.

I'm tired. Jim comes to comfort me.
*Look*, he says, *you're a businesssman.
It is easy for the camel to pass halfway
through the needle.
Clouds scorn the hunter who approaches
on borrowed wings.
The good man is blown about by every wind.
Peace is inner aimlessness.*

My soul enters a translucent room.
I move with a desire that knows no direction.
Slowly I make my way
around the face of a broken clock.

Jim drops by and says,
*Now you are getting somewhere.*

**SHADOW BOXING**


I have just been decked.
Jim says, *Lucky punch.*
I get up. My black image gets up,
pretends he's my brother.
He dresses in my clothes,
drinks my cup of coffee,
and drives off on my bear.

Jim says, *He'll be back.*
And I wait.
My eyes lose their color.
I am naked. My flesh dries
and I dream of the sea.
At night I crawl over
the broken glass
aching for a fight

Jim says, *He's back.*
And so we move around the room.
Snakes coil around us as we dance.
I pour oil over my body.
Now we are fighting
as we always have.

My fists are burning coals.
His arms are the branches
of great trees.
He offers me the city.
I offer him my costume.

Forever we move around the room.
I know I must give him a name.
Jim says, *Tomorrow.*

**Don Cushman** — is poet, printer, editor of *Cloud Marauder*, and Administrative Director of the West Coast Print Center.